PICTURE BOOK OF

NEBRASKA

By
BERNADINE BAILEY

Pictures by
KURT WIESE

ALBERT WHITMAN AND COMPANY
CHICAGO   ILLINOIS

Published simultaneously
in the Dominion of Canada
by George J. McLeod, Ltd., Toronto

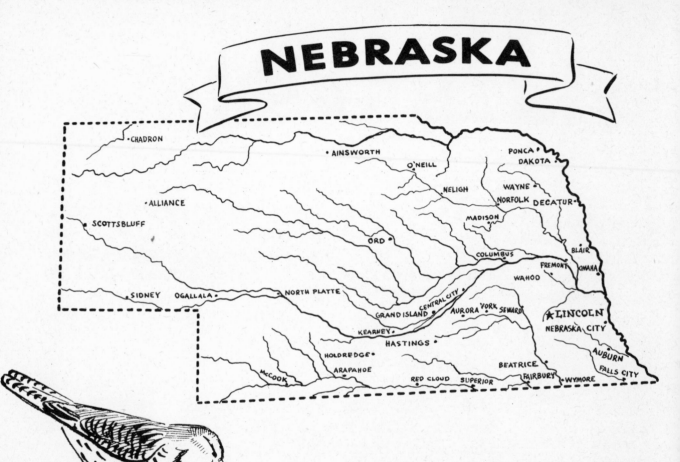

NEBRASKA

CHADRON
AINSWORTH
PONCA
O'NEILL
DAKOTA
NELIGH
WAYNE
ALLIANCE
NORFOLK
DECATUR
MADISON
SCOTTSBLUFF
ORD
COLUMBUS
BLAIR
FREMONT
OMAHA
WAHOO
SIDNEY   OGALLALA
NORTH PLATTE
CENTRAL CITY
★ LINCOLN
GRAND ISLAND
AURORA   YORK   SEWARD
NEBRASKA CITY
KEARNEY
HASTINGS
AUBURN
HOLDREDGE
FALLS CITY
ARAPAHOE
BEATRICE
McCOOK
RED CLOUD   SUPERIOR   FAIRBURY   WYMORE

WESTERN MEADOW LARK

INDIANS
CROSSING THE
MISSOURI IN
A
HIDE BOAT

Shaped like a giant flag fluttering in the breeze, Nebraska, the Cornhusker State, lies "out where the West begins." Its neighboring states are South Dakota on the north; Wyoming and Colorado on the west; Colorado and Kansas on the south; and Missouri and Iowa on the east. All its borders are ruler straight except on the east and a part of the northern border, where the winding Missouri River gives the state a crinkled outline.

With an area of 77,229 square miles, Nebraska is the fourteenth state in size. The Platte River, formed by the joining of the North Platte and the South Platte near the center of the state, makes a broad river highway from east to west. The Missouri and Platte rivers, with their many branches, provide waterways to all parts of the state. With canoes and flatboats, the Indians and early settlers made good use of these rivers.

Some four hundred years ago, the Spaniards who had settled in Mexico decided to extend their domain. In 1541, Coronado is supposed to have led a company of Spanish adventurers through the area that is now Kansas and Nebraska.

These men traveled hundreds of miles, by horse and by foot, seeking a city of fabled riches called Quivira. They found Indians, grass huts, and fields of corn, but no gold. These Spaniards were the first white men to visit this region.

Other adventurers and explorers came—Spanish, French, and English, but no permanent settlements were made. By the Louisiana Purchase of 1803, the area became the property of the United States.

When Lewis and Clark explored this region in 1804-1806, they found seven tribes of Indians: Pawnee, Omaha, Oto, Ponca, Sioux, Cheyenne, and Arapaho. Altogether, there were about 40,000 red men, speaking several different languages.

The Pawnee made up the largest tribe. These Indians lived in villages, where they built circular earth lodges, from 25 to 60 feet in diameter. Although they liked to hunt and fight, they were really farmers. On their small farms of less than an acre, each Pawnee family raised corn and beans, melons and tobacco. The squaws did the work.

The OTTER

A few Spanish fur traders had established trading posts in the region by 1802. Then in 1806, President Jefferson ordered Lieutenant Zebulon M. Pike to explore the region and to make friends with the Indians.

At a big council on September 29, Lt. Pike persuaded the Pawnee to give up their friendship with the Spanish settlers and to be loyal to the United States.

After this, the Pawnee got along very well with the white settlers. In fact, when the Union Pacific Railroad was being built, a "battalion" of Pawnee protected the workers from attacks by hostile Indians.

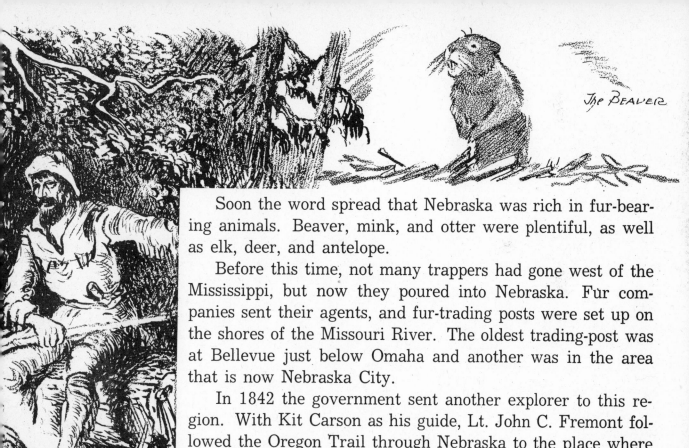

Joe Beaver

Soon the word spread that Nebraska was rich in fur-bearing animals. Beaver, mink, and otter were plentiful, as well as elk, deer, and antelope.

Before this time, not many trappers had gone west of the Mississippi, but now they poured into Nebraska. Fur companies sent their agents, and fur-trading posts were set up on the shores of the Missouri River. The oldest trading-post was at Bellevue just below Omaha and another was in the area that is now Nebraska City.

In 1842 the government sent another explorer to this region. With Kit Carson as his guide, Lt. John C. Fremont followed the Oregon Trail through Nebraska to the place where the Platte River divides.

In his official report, he commented on the Indian name for the Platte River. The red men called it Nebrathka—or Nebraska — which means Shallow Water. Because the name was so appropriate, it was given to the entire territory.

In the year 1844, a bill to create the Territory of Nebraska was introduced into Congress. It failed to pass because there were so many arguments about whether or not slavery should be allowed in the new territory. Ten years later, in 1854, a bill was passed that created two territories: Kansas and Nebraska.

Omaha City was chosen as the capital of Nebraska Territory, though many other cities fought for that honor. Francis Burt was appointed governor, but he died a few months later. Mark W. Izard became the second governor of the new territory, in February, 1855.

When Nebraska became the thirty-seventh state on March 1, 1867, the lawmakers again started to quarrel about which city should be the state capital. They finally chose the small village of Lancaster, a short distance south and west of Omaha. The name of the village was then changed to Lincoln.

Bit by bit the native Indian tribes were forced to give up their farms and their hunting grounds to the white settlers. Many of the Indians were sent to live on reservations, either in Nebraska or nearby states. Today there are only a few thousand Indians in Nebraska, most of them on the Omaha and Winnebago Reservations along the northeastern border.

When the newcomers saw the large herds of buffalo, elk, and antelope grazing on the rich grasslands of Nebraska, they knew this would also be a good land for cattle and sheep.

There was plenty of water for the animals, as well as shelter in the form of canyons, bluffs, and ravines. Transportation was the only thing lacking, and that was taken care of when the Union Pacific built a railroad here in 1867.

Even after the Indians had been subdued, life was still rugged for the early settlers. Ranchers fought among themselves for the best grazing land, each one wanting an area with plenty of water. Often they cut wire fences and carried on open warfare in order to get the land they wanted. It was a rough period, when the law was in the hands of the man who could shoot first.

Nature herself brought the worst hardships, from which there was no escape. Plagues of grasshoppers came at regular intervals, eating up the lush grasses on which the cattle fed. Blizzards of sleet and snow brought death to many herds in the winter of 1880-81. Discouraged and heartsick, many cattlemen gave up and went back East. Others lingered on, living on dried buffalo meat and trading hides for supplies.

When farmers came into Nebraska, more trouble started. The cattlemen wanted to keep their free grazing land to themselves. They fenced in large tracts of land, dug wells, and had all their cowboys take out homestead claims to as many acres as they were allowed. It was a losing fight, for the farmers outnumbered the cattlemen one hundred to one.

In spite of all the difficulties, however, settlers were attracted to Nebraska. Some came because they could obtain a farm so cheaply.

Under the Homestead Act of 1862, a man could claim 160 acres of land, live on it for six months, and then buy it from the government for $1.25 an acre. The Timber-Claim Act, of 1873, allowed a settler to obtain a 160-acre tract merely by planting trees on ten acres and taking care of the trees for eight years.

The Kincaid Law, passed in 1904, permitted a settler to homestead 640 acres instead of only 160. The free grazing land was now all gone, and

the reign of the old-time cattle kings was ended.

Instead of the enormous herds of Texas longhorns, smaller herds of beef and dairy cattle grazed on the pasturelands. Beef production became one of the principal industries of the state. It still is.

Large farms, each covering a square mile, made a checkerboard pattern of the landscape. Spacious farm homes, built of wood and painted white, replaced the crude cabins of the early settlers. Five railroad lines crisscrossed the state, bringing in factory goods from the East and taking back meat and farm products from Nebraska.

SHELTER BELT OF TREES
PROTECTS FIELD
& FARMSTEAD
IN YORK COUNTY
NEB.

Today, Nebraska is one of the greatest wheat-growing states of the Union. Like its neighbor Kansas, this state has the soil and the climate for growing winter wheat. Farms of more than a thousand acres are not uncommon, and in the summer the ripening grain ripples in the breeze like a golden ocean.

Corn is the second biggest farm crop, but much of it is fed to the livestock. Oats, clover, and alfalfa are also grown in abundance, both for local use and for shipping out of the state. About two million tons of wild hay are harvested annually in the Sand Hills area. Sugar beets have increased in importance during the last few years.

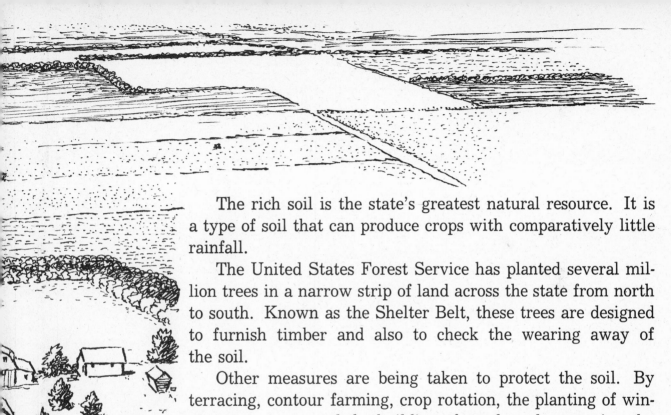

The rich soil is the state's greatest natural resource. It is a type of soil that can produce crops with comparatively little rainfall.

The United States Forest Service has planted several million trees in a narrow strip of land across the state from north to south. Known as the Shelter Belt, these trees are designed to furnish timber and also to check the wearing away of the soil.

Other measures are being taken to protect the soil. By terracing, contour farming, crop rotation, the planting of winter cover crops, and the building of ponds and reservoirs, the farmers hope to preserve their land and water supply.

Salt deposits were found in Lancaster County by the earliest settlers. This mineral was so rare that some people thought the national capital should be moved to Nebraska, to be near these valuable mines. The deposits, however, turned out to be not so great as it seemed at first.

Today, the chief minerals of Nebraska are limestone and clay, used for roads and buildings, as well as some chalk and shale. In 1939, oil was discovered and has grown into a large industry.

Omaha, with more than a quarter of a million people, is by far the largest city in the state. It sprawls for twelve miles along the west bank of the meandering Missouri River, directly across the water from Council Bluffs, Iowa.

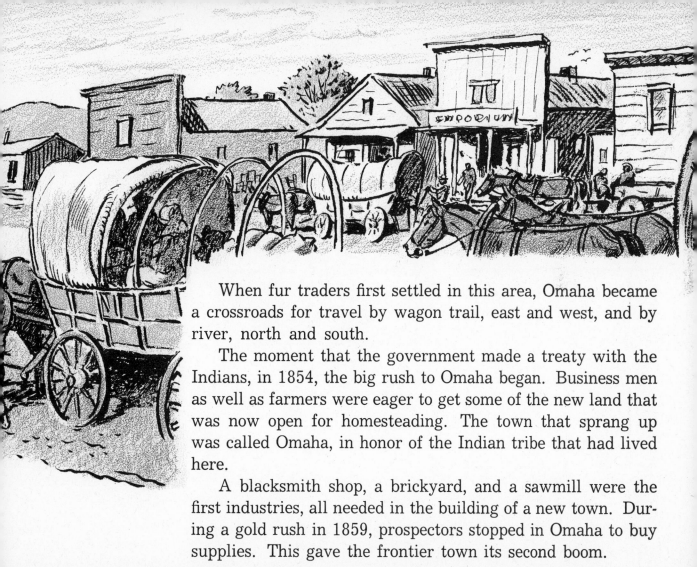

When fur traders first settled in this area, Omaha became a crossroads for travel by wagon trail, east and west, and by river, north and south.

The moment that the government made a treaty with the Indians, in 1854, the big rush to Omaha began. Business men as well as farmers were eager to get some of the new land that was now open for homesteading. The town that sprang up was called Omaha, in honor of the Indian tribe that had lived here.

A blacksmith shop, a brickyard, and a sawmill were the first industries, all needed in the building of a new town. During a gold rush in 1859, prospectors stopped in Omaha to buy supplies. This gave the frontier town its second boom.

With the coming of the Union Pacific Railroad, the steady growth and prosperity of Omaha were assured. Now the city could ship out the meat products, the corn and wheat and other grain, that were being produced throughout the state. When Council Bluffs was flooded, in 1881, many citizens moved to Omaha, which stood on higher ground. This gave the city another boom period.

Like the entire state of Nebraska, Omaha had its troubles in the 1890's. Grasshoppers and drought nearly ruined many farmers, and a financial panic nearly ruined everyone. The city survived, however, and continued to grow. As more and more people went west, Omaha became a trading center for farmers and cattlemen.

FLOW OF GRAIN FROM ELEVATOR INTO RAILROAD CAR

Here, they could sell their crops and cattle, which were held in the grain elevators and the stockyards until they were shipped East. Here, they could buy what they needed from the brickyards, iron works, flour mills, carriage factories, and department stores.

Many of the early settlers in Nebraska had come from Germany, Denmark, Sweden, Ireland, Italy, Poland, and other countries of Europe. Through club groups in Omaha, the descendants of these settlers have kept up many of their old national customs.

Creighton University has seven professional schools as well as separate liberal arts colleges for men and women. Given by the Creighton family and founded in 1878, it is administered by the Jesuits.

Omaha Municipal University, built by subscriptions from citizens, was established in 1909 as the University of Omaha. The Nebraska School for the Deaf offers twelve grades of regular school work to children who have defective speech or hearing.

The University of Nebraska College of Medicine was founded in 1881 as the Omaha Medical College. In 1902 it became a part of the University of Nebraska and the name was changed.

The Joslyn Memorial Art Museum contains many noted paintings and other art treasures. In its fine concert hall, the Omaha Symphony Orchestra presents a yearly series of concerts during the winter season.

On a hill ten miles west of Omaha is the world-famed Boys Town, established in 1917 by Father E. J. Flanagan. Almost nine hundred boys live here the year around in modern apartments and cottages. They receive both a grammar and high school education, with plenty of time for baseball, basketball, and other recreational activities. To more than seven thousand boys of every creed, Boys Town is home.

Omaha is known throughout the world for its huge meat-packing industry. Several big packing plants are located here, and at its Union Stockyards more than two million cattle are received in a single year. These animals come from many different states and as far away as Canada.

The city is proud of an organization with the name of Ak-Sar-Ben, the state name spelled backward. Made up of agricultural, charitable, and educational groups, the Knights of Ak-Sar-Ben annually present at their own field a World Championship Rodeo, a 4-H Baby Beef contest, racing meets, and other outstanding entertainment features.

Lincoln, the capital and next largest city, is in southeastern Nebraska, about fifty miles from the Missouri River. Settlers were first attracted here by the marshy flats of glistening white salt.

The state capitol, with its central tower rising 400 feet, is a striking example of modern architecture. It was designed by Bertram Grosvenor Goodhue so that it could be seen for many miles across the prairie. The building and grounds occupy four city blocks.

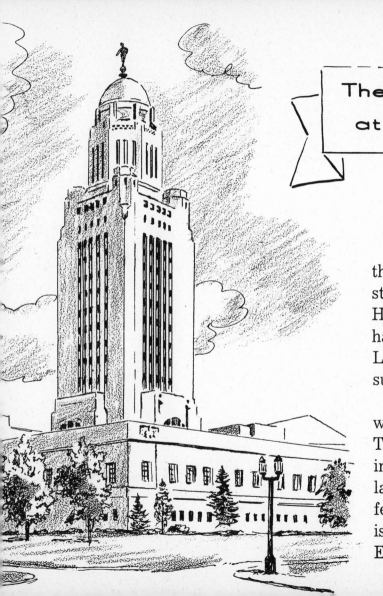

The State Capitol at LINCOLN

The sessions of the Legislature at the capitol are unique. Unlike other state bodies with both a Senate and House of Representatives, Nebraska has only a One-House or Unicameral Legislature. It is the only state with such a governing body.

Because of its colleges, Lincoln is well known as an educational center. The University of Nebraska, founded in 1869, is both the oldest and the largest. The University has ten different colleges, but special emphasis is put upon those of Agriculture and Engineering.

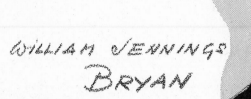

WILLIAM JENNINGS
BRYAN

The College of Agriculture, founded in 1874, grew very slowly. Today it does important work with 4-H Clubs, farm demonstrations, and original research in the Agricultural Experiment Station.

There is one name above all others that is associated with the city of Lincoln: William Jennings Bryan. He came here as a young lawyer in 1887 and was elected to Congress. He ran for president in 1896 and in 1900 and was twice defeated.

In 1900 Bryan returned to Lincoln and founded a weekly paper, THE COMMONER. He became famous as a speaker throughout the Middle West. In 1908 he again ran for president and was for the third time defeated. Bryan used to address great crowds of people from the balcony of his home at 1625 D Street.

GENERAL
PERSHING

CHARLES G.
DAWES

Two other famous Americans lived in Lincoln during this same period. Charles G. Dawes, who was Vice-president under President Coolidge, had a law office in the same building as Bryan. General of the Army John J. Pershing, the great general of World War I, taught military science at the University of Nebraska.

The city of Grand Island, north of the Platte River in the southeastern quarter of the state, was laid out by the Union Pacific along its railroad tracks.

Grand Island had one of the first beet-sugar factories in this country. This and several other small factories furnish employment to several hundred. Henry Fonda, the well known stage and screen star, was born in Grand Island.

A short distance south of Grand Island is the city of Hastings, founded by a group of Englishmen in the 1870's. The town was named for the man who graded the last section of the St. Joseph and Denver Railroad, when it was extended to this small village. Hastings grew rapidly after it became the county seat of Adams County, in 1877.

The brick clay found in this area became the basis for a thriving brick industry. Since the town was the center of a large farming area, plants making farm machinery and equipment of all kinds were built. These plants processed the farmers' products in flour and feed mills, in creameries and meat-packing plants.

Hastings College, organized in 1882, has an 82-acre campus and more than a thousand students.

North Platte lies in the delta near the point where the North and South Platte rivers join. It is a railroad town and trading center, with a much more western atmosphere than Hastings or Grand Island. Buffalo Bill's ranch was not far from here, and Cody Park was named in his honor.

Fremont, named for John C. Fremont, lies on the north bank of the Platte River, thirty miles west of Omaha. It has several small factories and is a trading center for the nearby farmers.

Midland College, which was moved here from Kansas in 1919, was so named because it is near the geographical center of the United States. The famous sculptor, Gutzon Borglum, studied in the Fremont schools.

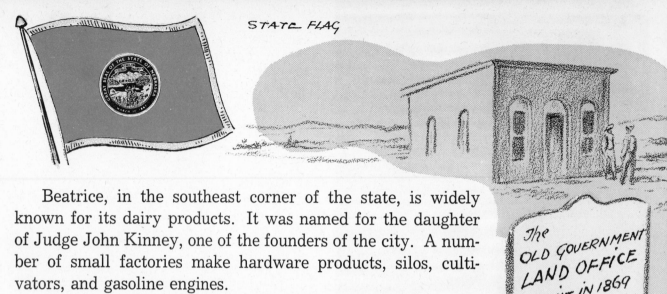

STATE FLAG

The
OLD GOVERNMENT
LAND OFFICE
BUILT IN 1869
WHERE PEOPLE
FILED FOR
HOMESTEADS

Beatrice, in the southeast corner of the state, is widely known for its dairy products. It was named for the daughter of Judge John Kinney, one of the founders of the city. A number of small factories make hardware products, silos, cultivators, and gasoline engines.

Just west of the city is the first homestead in the United States. The Homestead Act of 1862 became effective on the first day of 1863, and shortly after midnight of January 1, Daniel Freeman took up his claim to this homestead. His property is now a national monument.

South of Omaha on the Missouri River is Nebraska City, founded in 1854. It is a busy commercial center of a livestock area. J. Sterling Morton, Secretary of Agriculture under President Cleveland, made his home here, and started one of Nebraska's first newspapers, the NEBRASKA CITY NEWS. He also originated Arbor Day. His beautiful home, Arbor Lodge, is now a state park.